VOICE
MAGIC

VOICE

M^AG_IC

SECRETS OF VENTRILOQUISM & VOICE CONJURING

BY ORMOND McGILL

DRAWINGS BY ANNE CANEVARI GREEN

THE MILLBROOK PRESS • BROOKFIELD, CONNECTICUT

Library of Congress Cataloging-in-Publication Data

McGill, Ormond.
Voice magic : secrets of ventriloquism and voice
conjuring / by Ormond McGill.
p. cm.
Includes index.
Summary: Introduces the art of ventriloquism,
describing how to create the illusion of sound
coming from a vent dummy, a buzzing bee, a saw,
and a person in a closet.
ISBN 1-56294-137-2
1. Ventriloquism—Juvenile literature.
2. Conjuring—Juvenile literature.
[1. Ventriloquism.
2. Magic tricks.] I. Title.
GV1557.M43 1992
793.8′9—dc20   91-21000 CIP AC

CONTENTS

VOICE
MAGIC

WHAT
IS VENTRILOQUISM?

Ventriloquism is an entertainment based on verbal deception. It is the skill of misleading the listener as to the source of sounds. The ventriloquist suggests to the audience that the sound they hear next will come from somebody or something other than the performer.

Many people believe that ventriloquism is a special gift. Actually, it is not. Anyone who takes the time can learn to do it.

This book will teach you how to perform Voice Magic. In the first part, you will learn how to cultivate a ventriloquial voice and how to work with a ventriloquial, or vent, dummy.

In the second part, you will be taken deeper into the art of Voice Magic. You will learn how to apparently throw your voice at a distance, and you'll be let in on the great secrets of voice conjuring.

In the third part, some very interesting and clever vocal imitations will be revealed to you. You will amaze and amuse your friends.

Finally, you'll be shown exercises that will increase your mastery of Voice Magic. To master the craft, you need only follow the instructions, use your imagination, and practice, practice, practice.

ORMOND McGILL

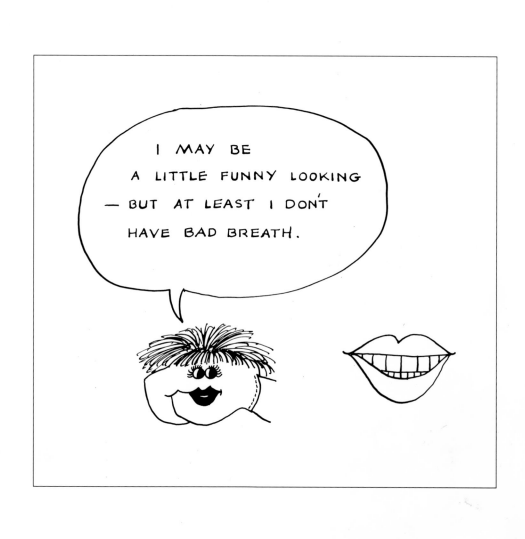

CULTIVATING
A VENT VOICE

Near Ventriloquism is the act of working with a vent dummy and appearing to make the figure talk. To learn how to do this, you need to develop a vent voice and an original speaking voice for the dummy.

Begin cultivating your vent voice by making sounds in your throat as you inhale deeply. Exhale your breath slowly through your vocal cords to produce a continuous, throaty groan. Experiment until the groan becomes a clear, even tone. Then, learn to raise and lower the pitch of this groan. This groan will become the basis for your Near Voice Magic way of speaking.

The vent voice originates well back in the throat. Ventriloquists usually choose a rather high pitched voice for the dummy. This voice provides a good contrast between their natural speaking voice and that of the dummy.

■ 13

After you have decided on the tone you intend to use for your ventriloquial voice, practice speaking words in it, and soon you will have perfected the dummy voice.

Once you have cultivated your new vent voice, the next step is to learn to use it without moving your lips. This takes a while, but you'll get the knack quickly if you keep your back teeth clenched together and let your lips rest slightly apart when you talk.

Try to say each letter of the alphabet in your vent voice without moving your lips. You'll find that most of the letters are easy enough but that it requires lip movement to form the letters *b, m,* and *p.* Although a seasoned ventriloquist can cover this difficulty with a slight movement of the head when pronouncing these letters, it may be best for you to avoid these tricky letters until you're more at home with your new skill.

Next, try speaking complete words without making any lip movement at all. Try out your vent voice by reading a book or the newspaper out loud. Don't get discouraged! It takes a while to master the craft.

You can be the judge of when you're comfortable enough with your new voice to take on the next challenge: manipulating a vent dummy while you speak.

MAKING A
VENT DUMMY

Ventriloquism has become a popular form of entertainment, so you can often find small vent dummies in toy stores. For a full-sized professional figure, you'd have to go to a magic shop. Or, as will be explained in a moment, you can make a vent dummy at home with a white glove, a bit of paint, and some yarn.

Store-bought vent dummies have a special string running out their backsides. This string is attached to a mechanism inside the figure. When you pull down on the string, the dummy opens its mouth. When you release the string, an interior spring causes the dummy's mouth to close. During a performance, the figure is often seated on the ventriloquist's knee. The performer talks to it, and the dummy appears to answer.

You may have difficulty referring to your vent dummy as an "it" because in operation the dummy is so lifelike, it seems

to take on a personality all its own. The more you treat the dummy as a living person with whom you are having a conversation, the more convincing the Voice Magic becomes. Giving the dummy a personality is what makes ventriloquism such fantastic fun.

As you work with the dummy, put animation into the figure. Move it about as it sits on your knee. When the dummy speaks to you, turn its head so it looks at you. When you speak to the dummy, look right into its eyes. It can squirm, seem restless, jump with surprise, shake with laughter, and do all sorts of natural things a living person can do. Some professional dummies even have special movements built into them, such as rolling the eyes from side to side in disbelief or lifting the upper lip in a scowl.

It's simple to make your own vent dummy, instead of buying one at the store. This type of dummy is called a glove dummy. Pull a white glove over your hand. Make a fist, then paint a face, putting the lips where your thumb and forefinger meet. The movement of your thumb makes the lips move.

To make a boy glove dummy, sew some black or yellow yarn on the top of

the white glove to make the hair. Paint the eyes black so they will stand out, and the lips red. Make the lips bright red so that as the thumb moves up and down, the audience can easily see that the figure is apparently talking.

To make a glove dummy with a female face, use strings of yarn to hang down as the hair, and paint the features to look like a girl, exaggerating the eyelashes and the bow of the lips.

You will be surprised at how lifelike a glove dummy can be once you learn to operate it smoothly. You can make the

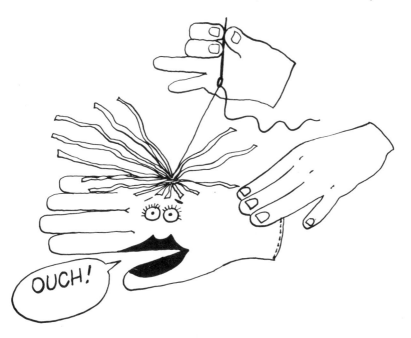

face change expression as you move your hand inside the glove. The red lips painted on the glove make a perfect mobile mouth for the dummy. All it takes is a movement of your thumb to give it a tight-lipped look of disapproval or a wide-open expression of surprise.

The ventriloquist Jay Marshall has made a reputation for himself by using such a glove figure. He created a glove in the form of a rabbit's head and named it Lefty, since he works it with his left hand. Internationally known ventriloquist Shari Lewis uses a glove in the form of a little sheep she calls Lamb Chop. She even sewed a sheeplike body to the glove to enlarge the figure a bit.

Use your ingenuity to create a unique glove dummy. And don't forget to give your dummy a name. At first, you may think it odd to give the figure a name and talk to yourself, but once you get used to it, you will find you forget it isn't alive; you'll even begin to believe you are speaking to another person. The more you create a separation between yourself and the dummy in which each of you becomes an individual in your own right, the better the near ventriloquist you will become.

PERFORMING WITH
A VENT DUMMY

What you make the vent dummy say is up to you. Just be sure it's entertaining. This isn't too difficult, because the novelty of the dummy's speaking is funny in itself. Usually the ventriloquist and the dummy engage in a comic dialogue.

Address the dummy in your natural voice just as if you were talking to a real person. When the dummy answers you, use your vent voice without lip movement while simultaneously opening and closing the dummy's mouth as you speak, so that the mouth movements coincide exactly with the words the dummy is supposed to be saying. Don't forget to keep your own lips motionless when the dummy is talking!

A good tip in learning ventriloquism is to practice in front of a mirror so you can watch yourself perfect the illusion. Once the technique has become second nature, proceed to animate the dummy.

It can squirm, cock its head inquiringly, look disgusted, or laugh at your jokes. If you treat your dummy as if it were really human, your audience will accept it as a person. The illusion of ventriloquism is so remarkable that even when people actually know better, they still can't help but almost believe that the dummy is alive.

However, the audience knows, of course, that it is you who is really doing the talking, even if the illusion of the dummy's voice is convincing. So when you add remarks made by the dummy that belittle you, the audience gets a big kick out of the joke.

Now, proceed to carry on a conversation with the glove dummy, using a comedy dialogue you have memorized. Here is an example of a ventriloquial performance you can learn by heart:

Have the spectators sit a respectful distance in front of you so the illusion will be effective. Enter carrying the glove dummy on your hand and turn to face the audience. Move the figure about a bit to get the audience's attention. Speak to the dummy and tell it to stop squirming. Now the fun begins.

YOU: *Well, Shorty, now that we're here, what do you say to everybody?*

SHORTY: *I don't know, you're doing all the talking!*

YOU: *Now, don't be a wise guy. What do you say?*

SHORTY: *Good evening, Gentlemen and Ladies.*

YOU: *Now wait a minute, Shorty. Don't you mean Ladies and Gentlemen?*

SHORTY: *No, I mean Gentlemen and Ladies. This year the ladies are after the gentlemen. Ha, Ha!* (Use a funny little laugh for the dummy.)

YOU: *That's enough, young man. Did you arrive in town today?*

SHORTY: *Yes, I just flew in from* [name a city], *and boy are my arms tired! Ha, Ha!*

YOU: *I'm getting sick and tired of you laughing at your own silly jokes.*

SHORTY: *Well, why don't you cut it out then? You're the one who's doing the laughing. Ha, Ha!*

YOU: *I think you're trying to make a fool out of me.*

SHORTY: *You sure don't need any help. Ha, Ha, Ha!*

YOU: *Come now, that's enough. Let's discuss something more serious, such as your studies. What are you taking at school, Shorty?*

SHORTY: *Oh, books, pencils, anything I can get my hands on.*

YOU: *Don't tell me that you steal!*

SHORTY: *All right, I won't tell you.*

YOU: (exasperated) *Just for that, young man, I won't let you talk to these nice people anymore.*

SHORTY: *That's okay by me. We're all tired of listening to you anyway.*

Pick up the figure and walk, as if angry, out of the room, with Shorty laughing as you go.

That's how it's done. Now, make up your own comedy dialogues. It's easy. Look through some joke books and tie the gags together into a smooth-running routine. Memorize them so you can deliver them with assurance. The laughs will come sure and loud. Even not-very-funny jokes become hilarious when the vent dummy says them in a saucy way. Banter with the dummy and let it get your goat. Breathe life into the figure. You'll love putting on a show as much as, or even more than, your audience will love watching you perform.

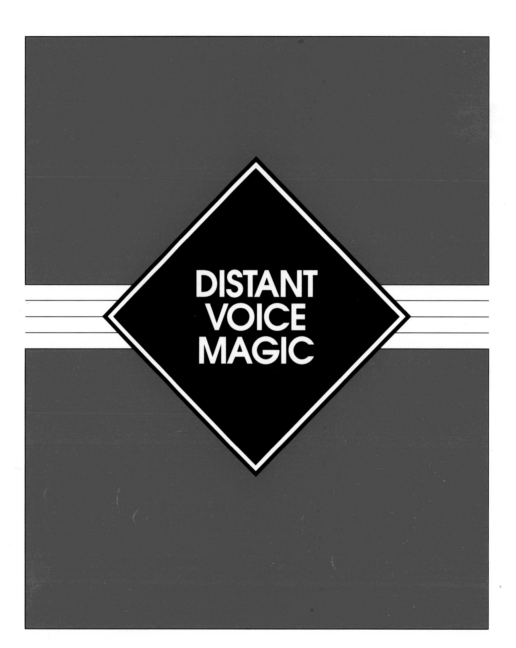

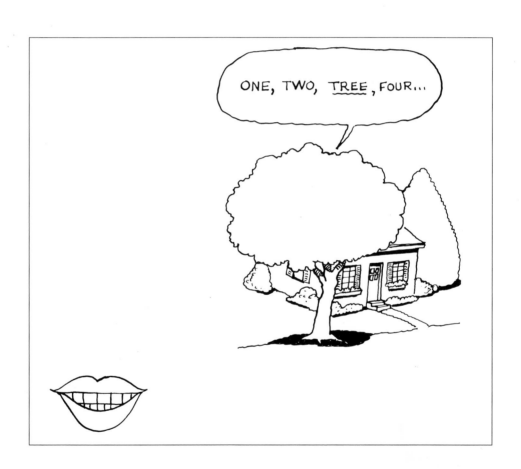

Near voice ventriloquism has become so popular that distant voice ventriloquism, in which the voice is apparently thrown into the room above, into the basement, or into a closet, has all but become a forgotten art. But it is in this form of ventriloquism that real Voice Magic is heard.

Actually, there is no such thing as throwing one's voice. Voice throwing is a complete illusion. That is to say, Voice Magic occurs when the ventriloquist produces a sound or a voice that simulates, or imitates, the way a sound or a voice would be heard if it came from a specific place. But it is the ventriloquist who has directed the attention of the audience to that place. This combination of artfully simulated sounds and the skillful direction of the spectators' attention forms the basis of the illusion.

We seem to make judgments about the kinds of sounds we are hearing and where they are coming from by relying on our past experience. For example, when we hear a certain familiar sound in the sky that grows increasingly louder and then gradually softer, we assume that an airplane has just passed overhead. We may even think we can tell what type of airplane it is, according to the speed at which the sound travels and the pitch of its engine noise.

It follows that if you can produce the sound of a person talking in the next room, even though you are right in front of the audience, the audience will perceive that sound as coming from a person in the next room. Of course, you have to imitate these sounds without lip movement (as you now know how to do) to make the illusion of voice throwing complete.

It is also important to understand that we use other clues to help us identify how far away sounds are, such as echoes and a lessening in loudness and clarity. The more of these factors you include in your simulations, the easier it will be to convince your audience that what you make them hear is really happening.

There is one more important element in creating a successful deception: auditory misdirection. In distant ventriloquism, sounds are produced in a different way from those you make every day. This is a trick that lets you fool the audience as to the origin of the sound.

This, in a nutshell, is the secret of distant voice ventriloquism. Next comes the mastery of this deception.

THE VOICE
AT A DISTANCE

Let's continue our discussion about distant voice ventriloquism by learning how to disguise the true direction of your voice. In normal speaking, you can't conceal the direction of your voice because sound travels to many points at the same time. In ventriloquial speaking, you form sounds in your mouth and throat in such a way as to confine the real path of the voice to a specific direction. To do this, compress your words, almost squeezing them out of your mouth, and turn your mouth so that it is at an angle to the audience. As long as the origin of the sound is not too close to the ears of the audience, there is no limit to the ventriloquial deception you can produce.

To produce this special kind of sound, press your tongue against your teeth. Direct your voice to the cavity between one of your cheeks. Use the air inside your mouth to make a sound, instead of

causing outside air to vibrate, which would tip the audience off to the direction from which your voice is coming. The sounds are also muffled and hollow, in imitation of distant voices. You can practice imitating distant sounds by having a friend go to the place from which you want the listener to think a sound is coming. Have your friend talk in a variety of ways. Listen carefully. Then, reproduce those sounds as closely as you can.

Now you need to learn to control the pitch and loudness of your voice. Loudness is determined by the amount of air that is pushed through your mouth. Pitch, or the highness and lowness of sounds, varies according to where you produce the sound in your throat. Practice making all sorts of different sounds—low and soft, high and soft, low and loud, high and loud, and everything in between.

There is another interesting fact about sound that you can make use of in your ventriloquial deception. People generally decide which way a sound is moving according to two pieces of information. They judge, for instance, that a car is coming up the hill on the left, passes by, then proceeds down the hill to the right by hearing the changes in loudness and

by the sound's passing from their left ear to their right one.

The ventriloquist can play with listeners' expectations by indicating the direction from which he or she wishes the audience to believe the sound is coming. You can do this by making such direct comments as "Are you up there?" "He's on the roof," or "He's in the cellar." Also, you can indirectly suggest the direction from which a sound is coming by looking in a certain direction or by turning toward the point from which you apparently expect the sound to come.

In this way, even before the sound is heard, the audience expects it to come from a suggested direction. Then, when you direct the sound so that it doesn't vibrate as usual in the listeners' ears, they have no way of judging where it is coming from. Add to these tricks your imitation of muffled sounds as though they are originating at a distance and your lack of lip movement, and the effect is amazing.

Practice producing the distant ventriloquial voice by keeping the pitch and the duration of sounds constant while gradually increasing and decreasing the loudness.

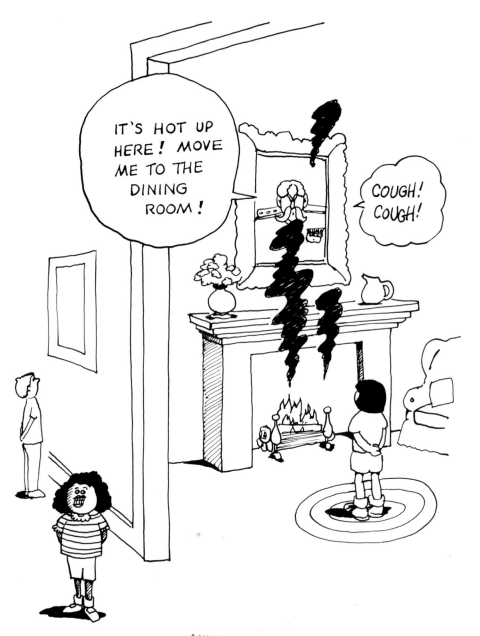

And remember, perspective is to the eye what ventriloquism is to the ear. You need to study sound in the way that painters study perspective on a flat canvas when they place shapes at different distances from the viewer. Listen for the actual effect of sound on your ears and then imitate that effect when you make sounds yourself. Your aim is to successfully render the illusion of sound for your listener just as the painter renders a visionary illusion for his viewer.

There are two main voices used for distant voice ventriloquism: The near distant voice appears to come from inside a closet or a box or from the other side of a wall. The far distant voice appears to come from the attic, the basement, or the roof. All this takes a while to learn. In the next two chapters, you'll learn how to produce each of these effects.

THE VOICE
IN THE CLOSET

You stand near a closed closet door. You knock on the door, and a muffled voice inside lets out a groan. You respond with concern, and you and the voice in the closet carry on a conversation.

To learn how to captivate an audience with this sort of ventriloquial performance, you'll need to follow these instructions very carefully.

Say a few sentences in your natural voice. Then, open your mouth and tighten your jaws. Draw your tongue back in your mouth and repeat the words you've just said. The sound, instead of being formed in your mouth, will come from your throat. If you hold your jaws rigid as you speak, the sound will resemble that of a voice heard from the other side of a door or through a wall.

To ventriloquize with this voice, stand with your back to the audience. Tap on

the door and call out in your natural voice, "Are you in there?" This will draw the spectators' attention to a person who is apparently in the closet.

Here is a sample of a conversation you might have with "the person in the closet." Concentrate hard on alternating between your natural voice and your ventriloquial one.

VOICE: *Yes, I'm inside. Please help me get out.*

YOU: *Okay, I'll let you out, but first tell me who you are.*

VOICE: *Please hurry, it's stuffy in here.*

YOU: *Well, who are you?*

VOICE: *I'm your friend Tom.*

YOU: *Tom! You can't be. He's on a trip to Europe.*

VOICE: *No I'm not. I'm right here in this closet. Open the door a crack and you'll see.*

YOU: *All right, I'll take a quick look.* (Open the door a crack and take a look inside.)

VOICE: (The voice is louder now that the door is slightly ajar.) *See, it's me. Now, give me a hand and help me out of here. I'm suffocating in this closet.*

YOU: (Slam the door shut.) *No, I won't. I don't believe you are who you say you are.*

VOICE: (The voice is muffled again from behind the closed door.) *Have pity and let me out. I'm choking in here.*

YOU: *Oh, all right. Here, come on out.* (Open the door and show the empty closet. Look at the audience in surprise.) *Why, there's no one in there!*

You can have any conversation you want with the person in the closet. The ven-

triloquial situation is so novel that almost any conversation with the voice will entertain your audience.

Note that when the door is cracked open, the tone of the voice changes accordingly. The voice, in this instance, must appear to come from someplace very near to you. To alter your voice for this effect, talk in exactly the same pitch and tone but produce the voice from another part of your mouth. Do this by closing your lips tightly and drawing one corner of your mouth back toward your ear. Let your lips open at that corner only. Since you are facing away from the spectators, they can't see this. Now, breathe the words out of your mouth and do not speak distinctly. Rather, expel your breath in short puffs at each word, as loudly as possible. This creates the illusion that your listeners are hearing the same voice they heard when the door was closed. However, the voice is more distinct and near to them.

This is the voice you will use whenever you want it to appear that the sound comes from someone close at hand but through an obstacle. You can use this same voice when you want it to appear

that someone is speaking from inside a closed box or trunk. Also, don't forget to modify your voice depending on whether the lid is open or shut.

When you perform distant voice ventriloquism, it is rarely necessary to show your full face to the audience. You may even turn your back entirely to the spectators in order to face the apparent source of the sound. Thus, your control of lip movements need not be as perfect as when you work with a vent dummy. This is an advantage, since it increases your flexibility.

THE VOICE
IN THE ATTIC

You look up at the ceiling and call out to an imaginary person in the attic. The person answers you! To the amazement of the audience, you carry on a conversation with this mysterious person.

You can choose to direct your conversation toward someone up in the attic or toward someone down in the basement, if you like. The key to this performance is that you stand with your back to the audience. Your mouth movements can then be less restricted when you speak in the voice of the distant person.

Be sure to direct the audience's attention to the attic by pointing to the ceiling and looking up at it. Call out loudly and distinctly in your natural voice. Ask some questions, as though you know there is a person up there. Remember that the success of the illusion depends on convincing the audience you believe in this imaginary presence.

■ 40

Now, in exactly the same tone and pitch of voice, make the distant voice answer. But, this time, form the words at the back part of the roof of your mouth. Draw your lower jaw back and hold it there. Keep your mouth open. Inhale deeply before you speak. Then, as you speak, exhale in little jerks, using a bit of air for each word. This will produce a sound that is subdued and muffled, just a little louder than a whisper.

You can make this distant voice appear to come gradually nearer, too. To do this, call loudly in your natural voice and say, "Come down here!" At the same time, gesture downward with your hand to increase the illusion.

Have the voice answer, "I'm coming," or "I'm getting closer now," being sure to speak a little louder as the imaginary person approaches.

Here is an example of a conversation you might have with a person who is up inside a chimney:

YOU: (Look up the chimney.) *Are you up there?*
VOICE: *Yes, I'm up here sweeping the chimney.*
YOU: *What for? The chimney has already been cleaned.*
VOICE: *I'm looking for birds' nests.*

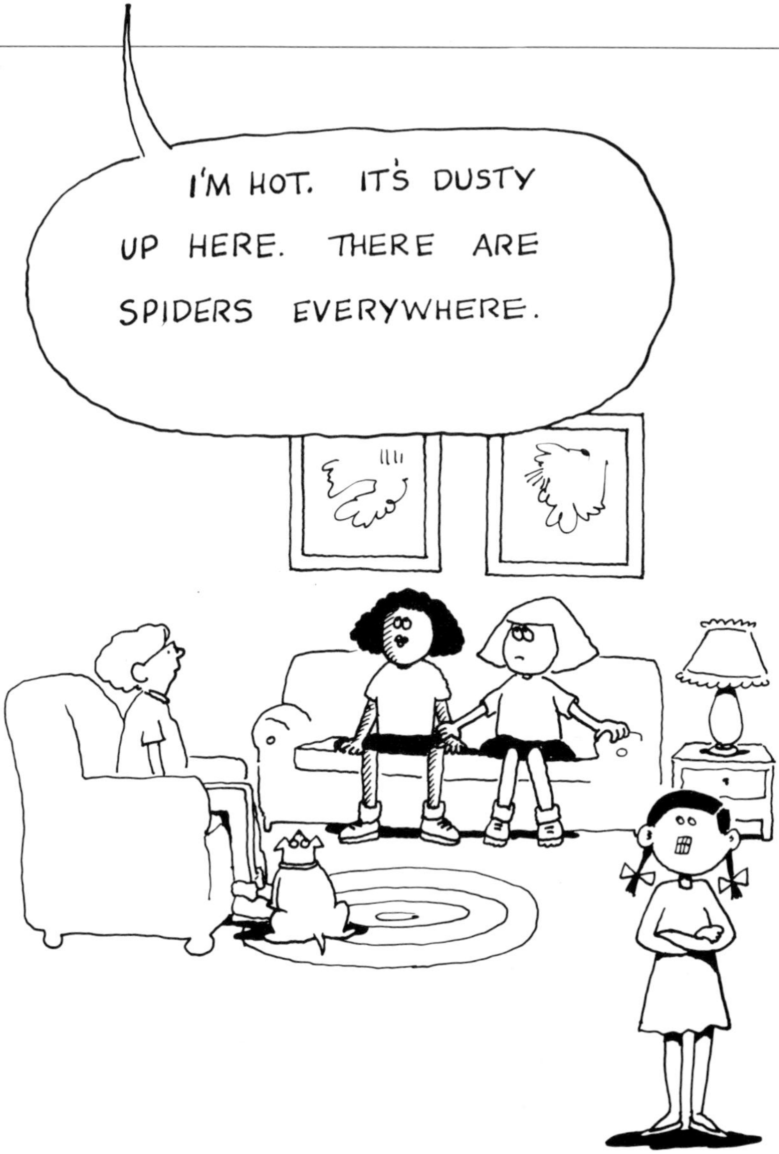
I'M HOT. IT'S DUSTY UP HERE. THERE ARE SPIDERS EVERYWHERE.

YOU:	*That's ridiculous! There aren't any birds' nests up there.*
VOICE:	*Dick says there are.*
YOU:	*Dick's crazy! Now, come down out of there.*
VOICE:	*No, I won't!*
YOU:	*You'd better, or I'll build a fire.*
VOICE:	(alarmed) *No, please don't do that! It'll get too hot.*
YOU:	*Okay, I won't. But come on down then.*
VOICE:	*All right. I'm coming . . . I'm coming.*

You can then continue your ventriloquial conversation with the voice as the person seemingly comes down the chimney. At every supposed step closer, alter the place from which the person's voice comes. Gradually open the cavity of your mouth and produce the sounds closer to your lips. You will create a larger space inside your mouth so that the voice will appear to come nearer and nearer by degrees.

By the time the person reaches the bottom of the chimney, your lips should be drawn into a circle, as though you were whistling. This enlarges the cavity of your mouth as much as possible.

Here is another conversation you could have with a man on the roof. Start by directing the attention of the audience upward.

YOU: *Are you up there on the roof, Frank?*

VOICE: *Hello down there! What did you say?*

YOU: (shouting louder) *I said, are you up there on the roof?*

VOICE: *I sure am. I'm putting on some shingles.*

YOU: *Good. Are you almost finished?*

VOICE: *I'm just putting on the last one now.*

YOU: *Fine. Please come on down then. I want to see you.*

VOICE: *Okay. I'll come right down.*

YOU: *Which way are you coming, Frank?*

VOICE: *Through the trap door on the roof and down the stairs.*

YOU: *How long will you be?*

VOICE: *Only a few minutes. I'll come down as fast as I can.*

Keep the conversation going as long as you wish. Make the voice get closer and closer, and use gestures to show that Frank is descending. Finally, as the voice approaches the door, speak in the near ventriloquial voice that you learned in the previous section. Practice hard, and the illusion will be complete.

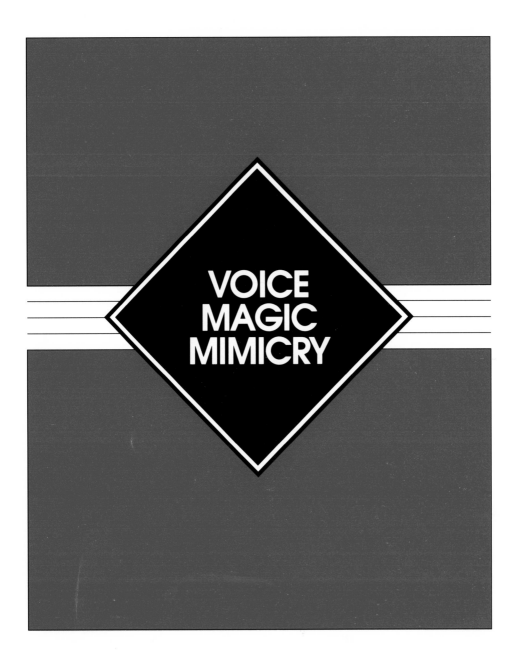

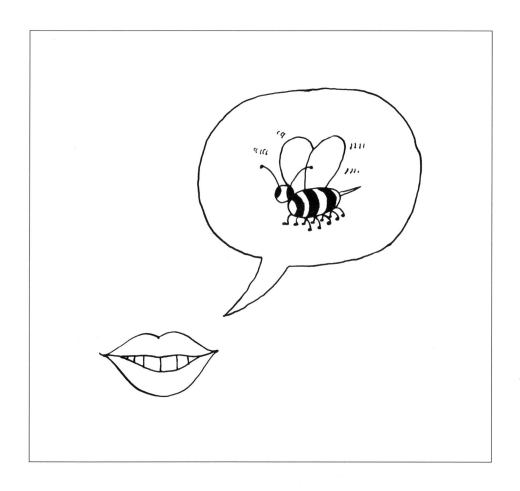

You can add to your ventriloquial repertoire by learning how to do vocal imitations. This is known as *polyphonic mimicry*. Audiences will marvel at your clever mimicry of sounds that are familiar to them.

When performing Voice Magic imitations, tell the spectators what you are imitating. Since they will then know what to expect, when you satisfy their expectations they'll appreciate your skills all the more.

Also, when you imitate the sound of a certain thing, include in your presentation a *pantomime reaction* to whatever the sound may be: Act as though the thing producing the sound is really there. For instance, imitate someone struggling to turn the crank to start an old-fashioned car while you mimic its clunking sound; bounce in your seat while the car chug, chug, chugs down the road; when a fan

is turning with a whir, imitate its sound while also struggling to stay upright in the gigantic wind it creates. The more you dramatize the situation associated with the imitated sounds, the more amusing your performance will be.

Making effective ventriloquial imitations depends on two basic elements: an understanding of the different effects sounds have upon your listeners, and a careful study of the types of sounds produced in the world by people, nature, animals, machines, and any number of different objects.

In the following chapters, you'll find out how to produce four very effective types of Voice Magic Mimicry.

CAPTURED BEE

The audience hears a bee buzzing around the room. People are usually scared of bees because they are afraid of being stung. So as the bee buzzes about, you act the part of a person trying to keep out of its way. Finally, you watch as it goes flying out the window. All is safe.

To imitate the buzzing of a bee when it is captured inside a room, put considerable pressure on your chest when you force the air out, as if groaning suddenly. Instead of letting the sound out naturally, try to confine it to your throat for as long as you can. The greater the pressure, the higher the faint sound you'll make. The sound will have a certain anxious quality that should perfectly resemble the buzzing of a bee flying around a room.

The audience will react to the success of your dramatization as well. When mimicking a bee—and all sounds, for that matter—start the sound softly at first,

until you find the right pitch. Then, boldly increase the loudness. In the instance of the bee, the insect should be heard to hum quietly at first and then to gradually become more and more agitated. It wants to get out. When the bee finally finds its way out of the room, watch it dart through the window. You might even go over to the window of the room in which you are performing and pretend to shoo the bee out. The bee is gone. Everyone, especially you, looks tremendously relieved. The point is, make the most of the situation.

BLUEBOTTLE

A fly can be a pest, and the bluebottle variety is the worst of all. It seems to delight in darting around you to annoy you as much as it can. Buzz, buzz, buzz— it flies all around your head. You try to shoo it, but it just won't leave. In desperation, you grab a flyswatter, and when the fly lands on the wall, you take a swat. A miss! More buzzing about, and finally it lands again. You take another swat, more carefully this time. Yes! This time you got the critter!

To imitate the buzzing of a bluebottle, make the buzzing sound just as you did for the bee, but this time make it with your lips instead of in your throat. Do this by closing your lips tightly—except at one corner, where you should leave a small opening. Suck air into that cheek and then slowly force the contained air out of the opening. Your lips and the side of

your cheek behind the opening will vibrate when you do this. If done properly, the sound will be an exact imitation of the buzzing of a bluebottle.

Play with the sound when you do this imitation. Follow the imaginary fly as it darts around. Produce bursts of sound as it comes in close to you. Try to scare it away with a sweep of your hand. Then,

gradually let the sound soften as the fly heads in for a landing. As you creep up on it with the flyswatter, it falls silent. Play a game of tag with the fly. Finally— whap! You got him! A look of blissful satisfaction spreads across your face.

CARPENTER

You tell the audience you're going to imitate a carpenter. Then, you give them a sampling of the kinds of sounds the tools will make. You put on a workshop apron and go to work. First, you mimic the sounds of the plane as the carpenter saws some wood. You pretend to pick up a plane and place it against an imaginary board. After the sound of planing has been clearly heard, you bring out some wood shavings and scatter them about.

Next, you put a board on the seat of a chair and rest your knee on it to hold it in place. You pick up an imaginary saw and go to work cutting the board in two. The sound of the saw can be heard ripping through the board. For a climax, you give the board a rap, and it breaks in two.

When you make the sound of planing, stand away from the audience and

appear to be pushing a plane back and forth. Produce the sound of the plane by dwelling on the sound "tsh." When you reach the end of your board, clip the "tsh" sound shut by pressing your tongue against the top of your mouth. Start the sound up again exactly when your plane contacts your pretend board, resuming its movement.

Repeat this sound over and over as you move the plane over the block of wood. When you're through planing, toss some wood shavings around to give your audience a touch of realism.

Now, it's time for the saw. To master this sound, take a saw and actually saw through a board. Listen carefully to its rasping. You reproduce the sound in your

throat. Note that there is one sound when you saw downward and another when you draw the saw up. Sawing is a back and forth motion, so make sure your sounds change to match the motion of your hands.

When you've apparently sawed the board in half, give the audience a surprise finale by cracking the board in half. This will be easy, since you will have sawed it almost in half before you began to perform. There's no need to mimic the noise of a breaking board. In this instance, you can let the board do the work.

ECHO

Here is a wonderful imitation for the close of your show. You turn your back to the audience and whistle several loud, short notes as if you were whistling for your dog. No sooner has the last whistle sounded than it comes echoing back to you. You then shout some words. They come back to you, too.

To produce a ventriloquial echo of your own whistling, whistle about a third of the number of original notes in the same pitch, as softly as you can. Remember to keep your back to the audience as if your attention is fixed on a distant place from where you hope your dog will appear.

You can produce a similar echo effect with shouted words. For example, say anything very loudly, such as, "Hello! Are you there?" Immediately bring your lips closely together and repeat the same

words in the same pitch, only much more softly. Form the quiet echo in the back of your mouth to get a subdued, realistic effect.

HOW TO BECOME
A MASTER

Any master ventriloquist has spent a lot of time perfecting his or her craft. The best way to practice is to talk out loud in a room by yourself. Make all sorts of contortions with the muscles of your mouth and jaws. Make sounds by pushing the air from your diaphragm (located between your stomach and your chest), from your throat, and from different parts of your mouth.

Fix your jaws in a rigid position, draw your lips in, and push them out. Notice how sounds are affected as you do this. Widen the opening of your lips and then draw your lips into a line. Listen very carefully to how sounds change when you alter the place from which they originate as well as the amount of sound you push out, the shape of the opening through which the air travels, and the actual pitch of the sound.

Study the real secret of the art of ventriloquism: to render sounds as they fall upon the ear. Then, learn to precisely mimic these sounds by expanding and contracting the muscles of your throat, mouth, face, and jaws.

During these exercises, inhale deeply and talk, first rapidly and then slowly, while you slowly exhale. Perform this exercise a dozen times in a row for several days. Take particular care to lower and raise the roof of your mouth, especially the back part.

All these exercises are ways to master the manipulation of sound so that you can cause your voice to appear near or far away. In other words, you are learning to give perspective to the sounds you produce. This is at the very heart of ventriloquism.

INDEX